A Precious Present.

From *Holy Mother Wisdom;*

as a reward of obedience to her word.

Brought by — Father William,

December 31st 1842.

Four Beautiful Diamonds,

These she said, I must place in this manner,

One on my Forehead, One on each shoulder,

and the other on my brest.

With this I received, her

Holy Love, and Blessing.

Mary Hazard.

SIMPLE WISDOM

Simple Wisdom

Shaker Sayings,

Poems, and

Songs

KATHLEEN MAHONEY

PHOTOGRAPHS BY LILO RAYMOND

DESIGNED BY BRIAN MULLIGAN

VIKING STUDIO BOOKS

*I would like to extend special thanks to Jerry Grant, assistant director
of The Shaker Museum at Old Chatham, New York,
for his kindness and his invaluable assistance.
—K. M.*

VIKING STUDIO BOOKS
Published by the Penguin Group
Penguin Books USA Inc., 375 Hudson Street, New York, New York 10014, U.S.A.
Penguin Books Ltd, 27 Wrights Lane, London W8 5TZ, England
Penguin Books Australia Ltd, Ringwood, Victoria, Australia
Penguin Books Canada Ltd, 10 Alcorn Avenue, Toronto, Ontario, Canada M4V 3B2
Penguin Books (N.Z.) Ltd, 182–190 Wairau Road, Auckland 10, New Zealand

Penguin Books Ltd, Registered Offices: Harmondsworth, Middlesex, England
First published in 1993 by Viking Penguin, a division of Penguin Books USA Inc.

1 3 5 7 9 10 8 6 4 2

LIBRARY OF CONGRESS CATALOGING IN PUBLICATION DATA
Simple wisdom : Shaker sayings, poems, and songs / Kathleen Mahoney : photographs by Lilo Raymond.
p. cm.
Includes bibliographical references.
ISBN 0–670–84808–5
1. Shakers—Miscellanea. I. Mahoney, Kathleen. II. Raymond, Lilo. III. Shakers.
BX9771.S536 1993
289´.8—dc20   92–50729

Printed in Singapore

Contents

Introduction

The Shakers are one of the oldest and most successful religious communal sects in the United States and, with one minor exception, the only one composed of native-born Americans of varying ethnic and religious backgrounds. "Tis the gift to be simple," sings one of the Shakers' rhythmic songs. Simplicity, hard work, and the love of God form the very core of the Shakers' existence.

In 1774, as America tottered on the brink of a war for its independence, a band of eight believers from Manchester, England, led by Ann Lee, who had assumed leadership of the group seven years earlier, first arrived at New York harbor in search of religious freedom. They were gentle, peace-loving people who believed in racial and sexual equality, love of neighbor, conservation of resources, and pacifism, a premise that, at the time of their arrival, brought suspicion and even persecution upon them. The group's formal name was The United Society of Believers in Christ's Second Appearing. The term *Shaker* was initially a derogatory one based on the group's frenzied dancing, which took place during religious meetings. As time went on, this behavior was replaced by orderly, rehearsed dances and marches done to lively songs. Eventually, the name Shaker became accepted.

It took two years for the small group to save enough to buy a plot of land in Watervliet, New York, near Albany. In 1781, Mother Ann, as her followers referred to her, set out in search of converts. Although she was to die without witnessing the establishment of the first "community in gospel order" in 1785 at New Lebanon, New York, through her teachings Ann Lee set the groundwork for a movement that encouraged charity, humility, temperance, and a simple life sanctified by hard work.

By 1800, the organization was firmly established, with Father Joseph Meacham having set down the Covenant of Constitution and written "Way Marks," a treatise that set forth the structure of authority and responsibility. The Millennial Laws, which governed every aspect of life in the community, were written in 1821. Each community was organized in self-sufficient units, or families, consisting of twelve to one hundred twenty men and women governed by an elder and eldress. Two to eight families made up a community.

Life in the religious community was highly structured and well ordered. Controlled by a central leadership and united by a single purpose, the community was founded on a dedicated work ethic. Labor was looked upon as a dignified, sacred commitment, providing the Society with direction, order, and a sense of unity. Ultimately, it was to bring the respect of the outside world. Following Mother Ann's directive, "Put your hands to work and your hearts to God," the Shakers raised daily toil to the level of worship. Their goal of perfection in all that was produced only encouraged their inventiveness.

The group believed in celibacy, yet there was no lack of children in the communities. Some arrived when their parents joined, while others were orphans adopted by the Shakers. Still others were indentured by their parents to learn a trade, which was fairly common at the time. Upon reaching twenty-one, each was given the option of joining the community.

In 1837, several young girls at Watervliet were seized with trances and visions. This was to usher in a period of renewal that rapidly spread to other communities. The first manifestations of these visions were the inspired songs and dances that members performed. Then, in 1843, drawings believed to be divinely inspired revelations from the spirit world appeared in dreams to a number of believers. These mystical images included a written description of the time, place, and circumstances of their creation. Early drawings were heart-shaped, but as time went on, decorative elements, many related to nature, appeared. Most were done at the Watervliet, New Lebanon, and Hancock communities.

Today, only a handful of Shakers survive, at the Shaker Village of Sabbathday Lake in Poland Spring, Maine. But in the mid-nineteenth century, the Society was thriving, with about five thousand believers in nineteen communities from Maine to Kentucky. After the Civil War, however, as factories reduced the demand for the Shakers' labor-intensive products and city life beckoned to many, their numbers started to dwindle.

The Shakers, with their genius for organization, excelled in business during the early decades of the nineteenth century. Known for their honesty as well as for the outstanding quality of their products, the Shakers had a thriving trade in seeds, herbs, oval boxes, brooms and brushes, barrels, cloaks, chairs, fabric, produce, medicine, and livestock, all of which were important sources of revenue to the communities. The Shakers were the first to standardize the ingredients in the production of pharmaceuticals and to package the seeds of fruits and vegetables for commercial sale. Today, however, they are best known for their spare, meticulously crafted furniture, admired for its functional design and its simple beauty.

The Shakers bequeathed us a legacy of enduring design. Yet to truly understand the Shaker spirit, it is necessary to look beyond these material objects to the less familiar but equally fascinating and insightful writings that speak volumes about Shaker beliefs and their way of life. The Shaker writings compiled here are timeless and eloquent in their simplicity. Taken from song books, journals, and official Shaker documents, many written more than one hundred years ago, these writings get to the very heart of the Society, encapsulating the profound yet simple truths we all recognize. Their down-to-earth philosophy is as appropriate and meaningful today as it was when it was first written.

Peace on Earth and good will to Mankind.

The Four Doves of Heaven, Bringing a blessing to Earth.

Poems

How sweet to have a friend so near and dear,
With whom you can as with yourself confer!
What joy can flow from thy prosperity,
If there's no friend that can rejoice with thee!
And in adversity, what pain of heart,
If there's no trusty friend to bear a part!
Friendship alone contains the noble art,
To soothe the wounded soul, and ease the Smart.

———

So much is plain beyond dispute,
That flesh is the forbidden fruit;
And those who may be so inclin'd
May propagate the human kind:
But, crossing the dividing line,
Between the human and Divine,
Of flesh and sense we must beware,
For Faith and Spirit govern here.

— *E. W.*
A Little Selection of Choice Poetry
Watervliet, New York
1835

To my dear Sister J. M. when away from home

Thou wert in my thoughts when morning dawned,
    And when the shades of evening closed around;
And when in dreamland's bright and pleasant walks,
    Our hearts together ever there were bound.

For Friendship true hath twined her silver cords,
    And golden links in pure affection wrought,
In strength of union are so firmly clasped,
    That mind to mind and soul to soul are brought.

And from my heart, there ever flows to thine,
    A deeper tide than words or actions prove,
And from thy soul there cometh unto mine
    Response sweet of sympathy and love.

        —Catharine Allen
        Mt. Lebanon, New York
        1888

To Sister O. H. Christmas 1892

Tho memories cluster round thee
    Of vanished years of life,
And things once loved and cherished
    No longer claim thy strife;—
Tho all that seemed the surest
    As phantoms glide away
The treasures of thy spirit
    Shall never know decay.

And now in twilight hours
    In silent vales of thought
Before thy inner vision
    Are scenes supernal brought;
While spirit friends are hovering
    To cheer and comfort thee
Till lifts the shadowy curtain
    To immortality.

—Catharine Allen
*   Mt. Lebanon, New York*
*   1892*

Smiles

A face that cannot smile is like a bud
that cannot blossom, and dries up on the stalk.
Laughter is day and sobriety is night and the smile
is the twilight that hovers gently between both,
and more bewitching than either.

—Anna White
Mt. Lebanon, New York
1865

Look not to the follies and pleasures of earth,
If you would inherit pure, heavenly mirth;
But travel in righteousness, meekness and truth,
And overcome all the temptations of youth.

—Anonymous

A blade of grass—a simple flower,
　　Cull'd from the dewy lea;
These, these shall speak, with touching power,
　　Of change and health to thee.

—From a Shaker seed and herb catalog
New Lebanon, New York
1833

A man of kindness, to his beast is kind,
Brutal actions show a brutal mind.
Remember, He who made the brute,
Who gave thee speech and reason, formed him mute;
He can't complain; but God's omniscient eye
Beholds thy cruelty. He hears his cry.
He was destined thy servant and thy drudge,
But know this: his creator is thy judge.

—Admonition posted in Shaker barns
Robert White, Jr.
Hancock, Massachusetts

The closing part of a Will ~ A Poem

Now sound of mind, and strong in health;
My will must stand the test,
To those who can esteem my wealth,
I leave all I possess.

In a preceding page you'll find,
My will in love is given;
Yet there's an Item still behind,
I leave my way to heaven.

You'll find it safe, there's no mistake,
'Tis yours at my decease;
And if this trying way you'll take,
You'll end your days in peace.

—*Issachar Bates*
New Lebanon, New York
c. 1832

Sayings and Directives

Behavior in Company

A man of words and not of deeds,
Is like a garden full of weeds;
Wherein no fruits or flowers grow,
But such as are both mean and low.

—Anonymous

Useful Instruction

He that is a chatter-box
    And chatters all the day,
Is like a bowl of milk that's skim'd,
    'Till nothing's left but whey.

—Anonymous

Table Monitor

What we deem good order, we're willing to state;
Eat hearty and decent, and clean out our plate;
Be thankful to Heaven for what we receive,
And not make a mixture or compound to leave.

We find of those bounties which Heaven does give,
That some live to eat, and that some eat to live,
That some think of nothing but pleasing the taste,
And care very little how much they do waste.

Though Heaven has bless'd us with plenty of food;
Bread, butter and honey and all that is good;
We loathe to see mixtures where gentle folks dine,
Which scarcely look fit for the poultry or swine.

> — *A Juvenile Guide, or Manual of*
> *Good Manners*
> *Canterbury, New Hampshire*
> *1844*

Labor to make the way of God your own; let it be your inheritance, your treasure, your occupation, your daily calling.

Do all your work as if you had a thousand years to live, and as you would if you knew you must die tomorrow.

> —*Testimonies of the Life, Character, Revelations and Doctrines of Our Ever Blessed Mother Ann Lee, Hancock, Massachusetts 1816*

Keep busy; idleness is the strength of bad habits.

> —*Fredrick W. Evans Mt. Lebanon, New York*

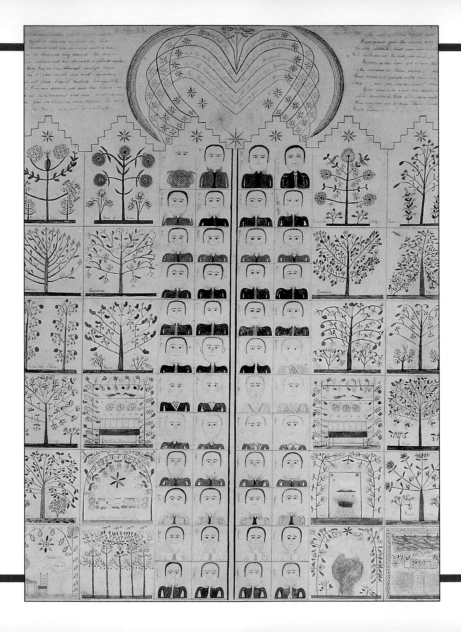

All that you do, do with your might,
Things done by halves are never done right.

—*Anonymous*

What people did not reason into, they cannot be reasoned out of.

—*Fredrick W. Evans*
Mt. Lebanon, New York

Wise is he who can take the little moment as it comes and make it brighter ere 'tis gone.

—*Daniel Orcutt*
Enfield, Connecticut

Be slow to anger, slow to blame,
And slow to plead thy cause.
But swift to speak of any gain
That gives thy friend applause.

—Mary Whitcher
Canterbury, New Hampshire

Better soil your hands than your character.

—Daniel Orcutt
Enfield, Connecticut

Flattery is a false coin which has circulation only through our vanity.

—Anonymous

Charity, like the sun, brightens every object on
which it shines.

—*Daniel Orcutt*
Enfield, Connecticut

Little acts of kindness which we render to each other
in everyday life, are like flowers by the way-side
to the traveler: they serve to gladden the heart
and relieve the tedium of life's journey.

—*Eunice Bathrick*
Harvard, Massachusetts

Forgiveness is as valuable to the one who forgives
as to the one forgiven.

—*Mary Whitcher*
Canterbury, New Hampshire

It is not the outside riches but the inside ones that produce happiness.

—*Daniel Orcutt*
Enfield, Connecticut

Our happiness is greatest when we contribute most to the happiness of others.

—*Harriet Shepard*
North Union, Ohio

The beauty of the world about us is only according to what we ourselves bring to it.

—*Eldress Bertha Lindsay*
Canterbury, New Hampshire

Take care of your thoughts and your actions
will take care of themselves.

> —*Daniel Orcutt*
> *Enfield, Connecticut*

True gratitude, like true love, must find
expression in acts, not words.

> —*R. Mildred Barker*
> *Sabbathday Lake, Maine*

The charity we extend others in the hour of weakness
will return at the time we most need.

> —*Harriet Johns*
> *Canterbury, New Hampshire*

Love, consolation and peace bloom only in the garden of sweet contentment.

—*Martha Anderson*
Mt. Lebanon, New York

As light is pleasant to the eye, so is truth to the understanding.

—*Richard Pelham*
Union Village, Ohio

Good temper is like a sunny day; it sheds a brightness over everything; it is the sweetener of toil and the soother of disquietude.

—*Anonymous*

It is a greater blessing to be censured when innocent than to be praised when undeserving.

— *Richard Pelham*
Union Village, Ohio

Miseries of Indolence

He who knows not what it is to labor knows not what it is to enjoy.

—*Anna White*
Mt. Lebanon, New York
1865

A selfish disposition knows not the sweet peace and contentment that flows from true benevolence.

—*Mabel E. Lane*
Mt. Lebanon, New York

He that is most positive in his opinions
may nevertheless be positively mistaken.

—Richard Pelham
Union Village, Ohio

Begin today! No matter how feeble the light,
let it shine as best it may. The world may need
just that quality of light which you have.

—Elder Henry C. Blinn
Canterbury, New Hampshire

Good works are the product of ripened thought.

—Antoinette Doolittle
Mt. Lebanon, New York

Justice is the only permanent foundation of peace.

—Catharine Allen
Mt. Lebanon, New York

Dew Drops of Wisdom

It is not any more justifiable to wound the spirit
than the body.

Vanity is a fruitful soil for every evil plant.

To be totally indifferent to praise or censure
is a real defect in character.

You may shine, but take care not to scorch.

Never promise more than you can perform.

Never forget the kindness which others do for you.

Praise no man too liberally before his face,
nor censure any man severely behind his back.

Keep your tongue and keep your friend.

The loquacity of fools is a lecture to the wise.

Speech is the picture of the mind.

The first step to greatness is to be honest.

The shortest answer is doing the thing.

Have the courage to prefer propriety to fashion.

Short-lived pleasures are often productive of pain.

It is the height of presumption to condemn things you do not understand.

Have the courage to hold your tongue, when it is necessary you should be silent.

He that lets the sun go down upon his wrath, and goes angry to bed, is like to have the devil for his bed-fellow.

Jealousy is nourished by doubts.

Truths like roses have thorns about them.

They that laugh at every thing, and they that fret at every thing, are fools alike.

A jealous person is a foe to himself.

Have the courage to speak your mind when it is necessary you should do so.

All truths must not be told at all times.

Never open the door to a little vice, lest a great one should enter too.

Revenge is a mean pleasure.

—Henry C. Blinn
Canterbury, New Hampshire

Gentle Manners

Labor to keep alive in your breast, that little spark of celestial fire called conscience.

—A Juvenile Monitor
New Lebanon, New York
1823

The Gospel Monitor for the Instruction of Children

Remember that the earliest age is the best time
to implant that which you wish to have thrive
or take deep root in children. And the present time
is ever the best time to correct a child for a fault,
even while it is fresh in its memory, and can realize
the justice of the correction.

—Mother Lucy Wright
Canterbury, New Hampshire
1841

Short Lessons of Instruction

He who broods upon his unhappiness, only increases it,
and makes himself more unhappy.

Conversation

Those who contradict others upon all occasions, and
make every assertion a matter of dispute, betray, by this
behavior, a want of acquaintance with good breeding.

Speaking of Yourself

Whatever perfections you may have,
be assured people will find them out; but whether they
do or not, nobody will take them on your own word.

—*A Juvenile Guide, or Manual of
Good Manners
Canterbury, New Hampshire
1844*

Songs

Simple Gifts

'Tis the gift to be simple,
'Tis the gift to be free,
'Tis the gift to come down
Where we ought to be—
And when we find ourselves
In the place just right,
'Twill be in the valley
Of love and delight.
When true simplicity is gained,
To bow and to bend
We shan't be asham'd,
To turn, turn will be our delight,
Till by turning, turning
We *come round right*.

—*Alfred, Maine*

Gentle Words

What the dew is to the flower,
Gentle words are to the soul,
And a blessing to the giver,
And so dear to the receiver,
We should never withhold.
Gentle words, kindly spoken,
Often soothe the troubled mind,
While links of love are broken
By words that are unkind.
Then O, thou gentle spirit,
my constant Guardian be,
"Do to others," be my motto,
"as I'd have them do to me."

—Polly Rupe
Pleasant Hill, Kentucky
1867

Love is Little

Love is little, love is low
Love will make my spirit grow
Grow in peace, grow in light
Love will do the thing that's right.

—*Anonymous*

May I Softly Walk and Wisely Speak

May I softly walk and wisely speak,
Lest I harm the strong or wound the weak;
For all those wounds I yet must feel,
And bathe in love until they heal.
Why should I carelessly offend,
Since many of life's joys depend
On gentle words and peaceful ways;
Which spread such brightness o'er our days.

—*New Lebanon, New York*
1869

Sunshine or Storm

Life is mostly what we make it,
Filled with sunshine or with storm;
Just whichever way we take it—
Sad or cheering—cold or warm;
Come what may, we need not borrow
Grief or trials, great or small—
Troubles of the brewing morrow,
Which may never come at all.

—Anonymous

A little Hymn, addressed to Youth

While blessings crown your youthful days
    With happiness and peace,
Let your good works declare your praise,
    And let your zeal increase.

And while you share this gracious part,
    (Good friends you are among,)
Let thankfulness possess your heart,
    And dwell upon your tongue.

Let not the sting of misspent days
    Be treasur'd in your store,
For Lo, how quick you've run your race,
    And time appears no more.

> —*A Juvenile Guide, or Manual of*
> *Good Manners*
> *Canterbury, New Hampshire*
> *1844*

Omniscience of the Deity

There is an eye that never tires—
    A God who never sleeps;
He knows the secret of each heart,
    A watch o'er us he keeps;
Beholds our motives, foul or clean,
    Knows we are mortals frail,
And yet we are upheld by him,
    His arm doth never fail.

We see in all his wond'rous works,
    The glory of his plan,
In giving agency to rule
    The final state of man.
As happiness depends on choice,
    We need not mourn or grieve;
Thank God he did our souls arrest,
    By this we did believe.

—Anonymous

Impartial Blessing

The little buds, may they be bless'd
    In doing as they're taught;
May they in loveliness be dress'd,
    And ne'er with frowns be caught.
I bless the hand that doth them bring
    In gentleness along,
That they may never feel the sting,
    For doing aught that's wrong.

The blooming youth, the tender vine,
    My blessing also share;
My spirit doth with theirs intwine
    With love and tender care.
Firm pillars may they yet be found,
    Within the house of God,
And may his praises by them sound,
    While moving at his nod.

—Anonymous

The Beasts of the Fields and Forests, both tame and
wild will be driven together and will beat peace with each
other; because of the destruction that will come on the
Earth; for it will come in the latter days, and they will
murmer and rebel against mankind; and shall not be
Tamed by man for a season

Reflections on Time

Time rolls away without delay,
No one can stop the wheels of time;
For time misspent we must repent,
We can't recall our misspent time.
Each day and hour gives its report
Of how we spend our time;
No age escapes, but in its courts,
Is shown the use of time.

There's no respect to age or sex,
But each one has their measured time;
God's gracious hand has the command
Of all our good and precious time.

He's bless'd us all with talents bright,
To use while here in time,
And as we sow, so shall we reap
When we have done with time.

—*Anonymous*

Speak Gently

Speak gently,—it is better far
  To rule by love than fear;
Speak gently,—let not harsh words mar
  The good we might do here.

Speak gently,—love does whisper low,
  The vows that true hearts bind;
And gentle friendship's accents flow,—
  Affection's voice is kind.

Speak gently to the young, for they
  Will have enough to bear;
Pass through this life as best they may,
  'Tis full of anxious care.

Speak gently to the aged Ones,—
  Grieve not the care-worn heart;
Their sands of life are nearly run,
  Let such in peace depart.

Humility

Humility, by nature free,
No law can her molest,
Altho the great and proud may hate
Her simple kind address.

Humility from lust is free,
And pride of every kind;
No bitterness in her address,
Provoking to the mind.

In quietness, we may possess
A meek and lowly mind;
For in her path, there is no wrath,
Nor ought but what is kind.

—*Anonymous*

Ode to Contentment

> Nothing on the earth below,
> Naught that heaven can bestow,
>   Fills the soul with peace,
> If Contentment dwell not there,
> All is dreary, dark and bare;
> She alone makes heavenly fare,
>   She alone is bliss.
>
> But content will not abide,
> In a soul puff'd up with pride;
>   Neither will she stay,
> With a soul defil'd with lust;
> Nor with him who is unjust;
> Him who covets, she'll not trust,
>   But will flee away.

> —*A Collection of Millennial Hymns*
> *Canterbury, New Hampshire*
> *1847*

Speak gently, kindly to the poor,
　　Let not harsh tones be heard;
They have enough they must endure,
　　Without an unkind word.

Speak gently to the erring,—know,
　　They may have toil'd in vain;
Perchance, unkindness made them so;
　　O! win them back again.

Speak gently! He who gave his life
　　To bend man's stubborn will,
When elements were in fierce strife
　　Said to them "Peace, be still."

Speak gently,—'tis a little thing
　　Dropp'd in the heart's deep well;
The good, the joy which it may bring,
　　Eternity shall tell.

　　　　　　　　—Anonymous

My Feelings

How joyful, how thankful, how loving I feel,
And still I want more love, yea more love and zeal;
I want my love perfect, I want my love pure
That I may with patience all things well endure.

I want to feel little, more simple, more mild,
More like our blest parents, and more like a child,
More thankful, more humble, more lowly in mind
More watchful, more pray'rful, more loving and kind.

—Anonymous

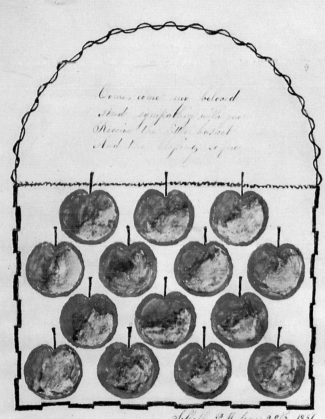

Come, come my beloved
And sympathize with me
Receive the little basket
And the dying ____

Sabbath P. M. June 29th 1856.

I saw Judith Collins bringing a little basket full of beautiful apples
for the Ministry, from Father Eleazer Rand and Mother Hannah Kendall.
as their blessing and love charm around the bail represents
the continuation of their blessing. I noticed in particular as
she brought them to me the ends of the stems looked fresh

The Union of the Spirit

Come old and young, come great and small
Here's love and union free for all;
And every one that will obey,
Have now a right to dance and play;
For dancing is a sweet employ,
It fills the soul with heavenly joy,
It makes our love and union flow,
While round, and round, and round we go.

—*Anonymous*

The Glorious Morn

O glorious morn! O happy day!
   Thy precious light, thy piercing ray
Dispels the darkness all away,
   All nature's on the move.

—*Anonymous*

Improve each Moment

Improve each moment as it flies,
Now in this blessed day;
So run that we may win the prize,
There's danger in delay.

This day, this hour may be the last,
For death is sure to all,
And not a single minute past,
Can any soul recall.
O Lord, may every breath be drawn
In prayer, in thanks or praise,
That I may say, when time is gone,
I've well improv'd my days.

—*Millennial Praises,*
Containing a Collection of
Gospel Hymns
Hancock, Massachusetts
1813

Shaker Communities

Watervliet, New York, 1787–1938
Mt. Lebanon, New York, 1787–1947 (called New Lebanon prior to 1862)
Enfield, Connecticut, 1790–1917
Hancock, Massachusetts, 1790–1960
Canterbury, New Hampshire, 1792–1992
Tyringham, Massachusetts, 1792–1875
Alfred, Maine, 1793–1932
Shirley, Massachusetts, 1793–1908
Harvard, Massachusetts, 1793–1918
Enfield, New Hampshire, 1793–1923
Sabbathday Lake, Maine, 1794–present
Union Village, Ohio, 1806–1912
Pleasant Hill, Kentucky, 1806–1910
Watervliet, Ohio, 1806–1910
South Union, Kentucky, 1807–1922
West Union, Indiana, 1810–1827
Savoy, Massachusetts, 1817–1825 (moved to Mt. Lebanon)
North Union, Ohio, 1822–1889
Whitewater, Ohio, 1824–1907
Sodus Bay and Groveland, New York, 1826–1895 (moved to Watervliet)
Narcoossee, Florida, 1896–1911
White Oak, Georgia, 1898–1902 (extension of Mt. Lebanon)

A Guide to Shaker Collections

Shaker Museum,
SabbathdayLake
Poland Spring, Maine
(207) 926-4597

Shelburne Museum
Shelburne, Vermont
(802) 985-3344

Canterbury Shaker Village
Canterbury, New Hampshire
(603) 783-9977

The Museum at Lower
Shaker Village
Enfield, New Hampshire
(603) 632-4346

Fruitlands Museum,
Prospect Hill
Harvard, Massachusetts
(508) 456-3924

Hancock Shaker Village
Pittsfield, Massachusetts
(413) 443-0188

The Shaker Museum
Old Chatham, New York
(518) 794-9100

Metropolitan Museum of Art
New York, New York
(212) 879-5500

Philadelphia Museum of Art
Philadelphia, Pennsylvania
(215) 763-8100

Durham Tavern Museum
Cleveland, Ohio
(216) 431-1060

Shaker Historical
Society Museum
Shaker Heights, Ohio
(216) 921-1201

Warren County Historical
Society Museum
Lebanon, Ohio
(513) 932-1817

Western Reserve Historical
Society Museum
Cleveland, Ohio
(216) 721-5727

Henry Francis DuPont
Winterthur Museum
Winterthur, Delaware
(302) 888-4600

Shaker Village at Pleasant Hill
Harrodsburg, Kentucky
(606) 734-5411

Kentucky Museum
Bowling Green, Kentucky
(502) 745-2592

Shakertown at South Union
South Union, Kentucky
(502) 542-4167

The American Museum
in Britain
Bath, England
225-46-0503

Notes on the Photographs and Artwork

Page ii: *A Bower of Mulberry Trees* (1854) by Hannah Cohoon. Photo courtesy of Hancock Shaker Village, Pittsfield, Massachusetts. **Page 12:** *Peace on Earth and Good Will to Mankind* by Miranda Barber (1919–1871). Photo courtesy of The Western Reserve Historical Society, Cleveland, Ohio. **Page 15:** Laundry room in the laundry and machine shop building (1790), Hancock Shaker Village. **Page 16:** View of the rear of the meetinghouse at the Shaker Village of Sabbathday Lake. The bell is from the dwelling house at Alfred, Maine. Photo by Kathleen Mahoney. **Page 19:** A blanket chest from Mt. Lebanon and a bucket from Canterbury at the Shaker Museum and Library, Old Chatham. **Page 20 (top):** Pitcher and bowl on washstand, Hancock Shaker Village. **Page 20 (bottom):** A tailor's counter from Mt. Lebanon and sewing items, carriers, and a basket from Canterbury and Mt. Lebanon at the Shaker Museum and Library, Old Chatham. **Page 23:** *Floral Wreath* (1853), Hancock Shaker Village, Pittsfield, Massachusetts. **Page 24:** Poultry house (1878), Hancock Shaker Village. **Page 26:** *Beloved Sister Anna . . . June 1853*, attributed to Polly Collins, Hancock. Photo courtesy of the Library of Congress. **Page 29:** *A Present from the Natives Brought by One of Father Issachar's Tribe* (1848), attributed to Polly Ann Reed, New Lebanon. Photo courtesy of The Western Reserve Historical Society, Cleveland, Ohio. **Page 30:** Ironware and buckets from Mt. Lebanon at the Shaker Museum and Library, Old Chatham. **Page 33:** Poultry house (1878), Hancock Shaker Village. **Page 34:** *An Emblem of the Heavenly Sphere* (1854). Photo courtesy of Hancock Shaker Village, Pittsfield, Massachusetts. **Page 37:** Curly maple chair with bird's-eye maple slats and pewter tilters (c. 1850) by Benjamin Gates, Mt. Lebanon, and straw hat (c. 1870) in the Shaker Museum and Library, Old Chatham. **Page 38:** Meetinghouse (1794) at the Shaker Village at Sabbathday Lake. Photo by Kathleen Mahoney. **Page 41:** Attic in the laundry and machine shop building (1790), Hancock Shaker Village. Photo reprinted by permission of *House Beautiful*, copyright [g] October 1979. The Hearst Corporation. All rights reserved. **Page 42:** Stencil from Mt. Lebanon at the Shaker Museum and Library, Old Chatham. **Page 45:** Herb house (1824), boys' shop (1850), spin shop, and wood house (1816) at the Shaker Village at Sabbathday Lake. **Page 46:** *From Holy Mother*

Wisdom. To Elder Ebenezer Bishop, attributed to Miranda Barber (1819-1871), Mt. Lebanon. Photo courtesy of the Philadelphia Museum of Art: Gift of Mr. and Mrs. Julius Zeiget. **Page 49:** Laundry room, Hancock Shaker Village. **Page 50:** Meeting room in meetinghouse, the Shaker Village at Sabbathday Lake. **Page 53:** *A Present from Mother Ann to Mary H.* (1848), attributed to Polly Ann Reed, New Lebanon. Photo courtesy of Abby Aldrich Rockefeller Folk Art Center, Colonial Williamsburg Foundation. **Page 54:** Elders meeting room, Hancock Shaker Village. **Page 57:** Infirmary, Church Family dwelling house (1830) at Hancock Shaker Village. Photo reprinted by permission of *House Beautiful*, © October 1979. The Hearst Corporation. All rights reserved. **Page 58:** Rocking chair and built-in cupboard, Hancock Shaker Village. Photo reprinted by permission of *House Beautiful*, © October 1979. The Hearst Corporation. All rights reserved. **Page 60:** *The Tree of Life* (1854) by Hannah Cohoon. Photo courtesy of Hancock Shaker Village, Pittsfield, Massachusetts. **Page 62:** *City of Pease* (1844) by Joseph Wicker, Hancock. Photo courtesy of The Western Reserve Historical Society, Cleveland, Ohio. **Page 64:** The ministry shop (1839, expanded 1875) at the Shaker Museum at Sabbathday Lake. Photo by Kathleen Mahoney. **Page 67:** Eldresses' bedroom in the ministry shop (1874), Hancock Shaker Village. **Page 68:** Round stone barn (1826), Hancock Shaker Village. **Page 71:** *A Golden Crown of Comfort and Rest from Heavy Sufferings* (1846): by Phebe Smith, Watervliet. Photo courtesy of The Western Reserve Historical Society, Cleveland, Ohio. **Page 72:** Elders meeting room, Hancock Shaker Village. **Page 75:** Union meeting room in the Church Family dwelling house (1830), Hancock Shaker Village. **Page 76:** *The Beasts of the Fields and Forests* by Miranda Barber (1819-1871), Mt. Lebanon. Photo courtesy of The Western Reserve Historical Society, Cleveland, Ohio. **Page 79:** Basket of split black ash, Hancock Shaker Village. Photo reprinted by permission of *House Beautiful*, copyright © October 1979. The Hearst Corporation. All rights reserved. **Page 80:** Horse barn (1850), Hancock Shaker Village. **Page 83:** Stocking forms, iron, and bucket at Hancock Shaker Village. **Page 84:** Meetinghouse (1820), Shaker Village of Pleasant Hill. Photo by Kathleen Mahoney. **Page 87:** *A Little Basket Full of Beauiful Apples* (1856) by Hannah Cohoon. Photo courtesy of Hancock Shaker Village, Pittsfield, Massachusetts. **Page 88:** Shaker dresses and chair, Hancock Shaker Village. Photo reprinted by permission of *House Beautiful*, © October 1979. The Hearst Corporation. All rights reserved. **Page 91:** Red barn at Shaker Village of Pleasant Hill. Photo by Kathleen Mahoney.

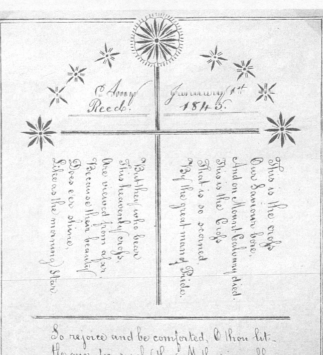

Amy Reed.

January 1st 1845.

This is the cross
Our Saviour bore,
And on Mount Calvary died.
This is the Cross
That is so seemed,
By the great many Pride.

But they who bear
This heavenly cross,
Are viewed from afar,
Because their beauty
Does ere shine,
Like as the morning Star.

So rejoice and be comforted, O thou little one, for surely thy Mother is well pleased with thee. And around thy neck does she place this bright golden cross, signifying that thou dost faithfully bear the cross of Christ.